MY FIRST ENCYCLOPEDIA

An eye-catching series of information books designed to encourage young children to find out more about the world around them. Each one is carefully prepared by a subject specialist with the help of experienced writers and educational advisers.

KINGFISHER
Kingfisher Publications Plc
New Penderel House, 283-288 High Holborn, London WC1V 7HZ

First published in paperback by Kingfisher Publications Plc 1994
2 4 6 8 10 9 7 5 3 1

1BP/0500/SF/(FR)/135MA

Originally published in hardback under the series title Young World
This edition © copyright Kingfisher Publications Plc 2000
Text & Illustrations © copyright Kingfisher Publications Plc 1992

ISBN 1 85697 268 2

Phototypeset by Waveney Typesetters, Norwich
Printed in China

People and Places

Kingfisher

Author
Dominique Rist

Translator
Pat Pailing

Series consultant
Brian Williams

Editor
Véronique Herbold

Designer
Anne Boyer

Illustrators
Graffito (maps)
Marc Lagarde
Barry Mitchell
Jean-Marc Pau
Etiénne Souppart
Valérie Stetten
Jean Torton

About this book

There are five thousand million people on Earth, and you are one of them! We all share one world, but we are all different. We may wear different clothes, or we may speak different languages and have different customs.

People live in places that look very different from one another. Some countries are dry and scorching hot. Others are wet but just as hot, or cool and damp, or cold and snowy. These differences affect the way people live – the clothes we wear, the food we eat and the homes we build.

This book takes you right around the globe, from the huge continents of America, Europe, Africa, Asia, and Australia to tiny islands in the Pacific Ocean. On the way you'll see people in particular communities – Inuits fishing in the frozen north, children playing on a city street, monks chanting in a mountain monastery, shearers at work on a sheep station. Each community is an important part of our fascinating world.

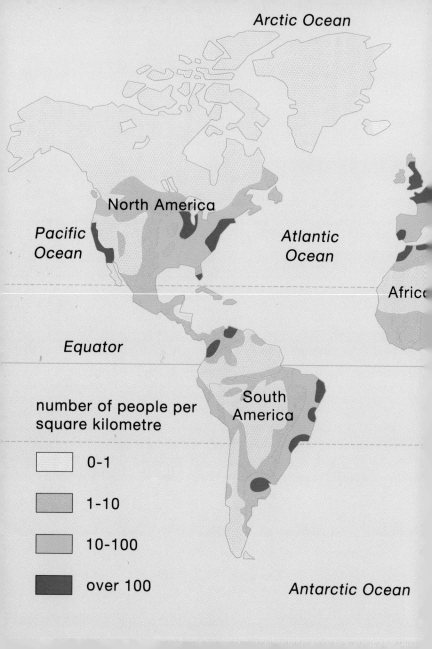

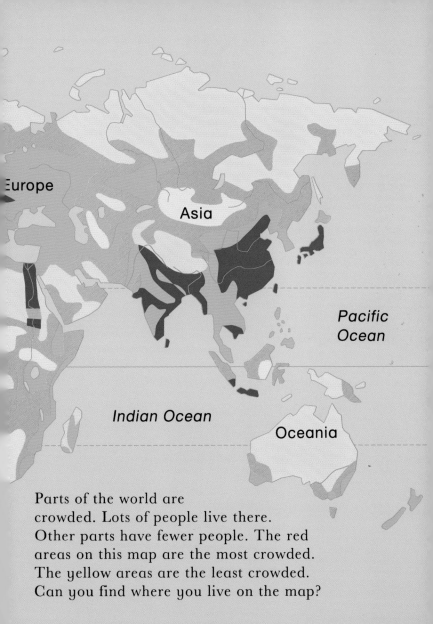

Parts of the world are
crowded. Lots of people live there.
Other parts have fewer people. The red
areas on this map are the most crowded.
The yellow areas are the least crowded.
Can you find where you live on the map?

CONTENTS

ASIA

OCEANIA

People
everywhere

Hello !

jamm nga fënaan

اَلسَّلَامُ ~ عَلَيْكُمْ

你好嗎

BONJOUR !

တမင်္ဂလာပါ။

تابق

नमस्ते

There are almost three thousand languages in the world. Many people speak more than one language.

Buenos días

здрáвствуй

שָׁלוֹם, בֹּקֶר טוֹב

আসুলেভো

günaydın

καλημέρα

안녕

おはよう

The words people speak and write may
sound and look very different. Here is how
to say "hello" in just a few languages.

Home sweet home

Arctic igloo

Indian tepee

Tuareg tent

Australian house

Borneo
longhouse

Benin
stilt house

cave
dwelling

Irish
cottage

Spanish
hacienda

People live in many kinds of homes, built of many kinds of materials, on the ground and on water.

Mongolian yurt

mobile home

Chinese sampan

Marsh Arab straw house

Mali mud house

Southern African hut

Mediterranean house

Venetian palace

skyscraper

17

Time to eat

People eat different kinds of food

Everyone gathers round in Arab countries,

You kneel on cushions in Japan,

in different places.

and in Africa.

and sit round a table in France.

Going to work

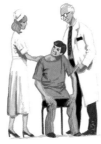

bringing
the news

looking after people

entertaining people

All over the world, the same jobs have to be done.

finding and cooking food

building bridges and tunnels

Sports

running

jumping

weight-lifting

basketball

tennis

American football

surfing

skiing

All over the world people
enjoy playing and watching
sport.

gymnastics   ice-skating   swimming

sumo wrestling   boxing

motor racing   horse racing

23

Religion

Christians believe in one God and in Jesus Christ. They worship in churches.

Jews believe in one God and in the Messiah. The Wailing Wall in Jerusalem is an important place of prayer.

Muslims believe in one God, Allah. Their religion is called Islam. Muslims go on pilgrimage to Mecca.

Hindu pilgrims visit the holy city of Varanasi. Hindus worship many gods, such as Brahma, Shiva and Vishnu.

Buddhists follow the teachings of Gautama, the Buddha. There are statues of him in Buddhist temples.

Shinto is the ancient religion of Japan. Shinto means "way of the gods" in Japanese. People worship many gods in Shinto shrines.

25

On the move

People travel all over the world,

They take a train, or a bus,

They cross the sea by plane,

on foot and on horseback, even by camel.

and they ride in a jeep or on a bike.

or in a boat.

Amazing facts

Every year there are millions more people in the world. In 1950 there were 2,500 million people. Today there are more than twice that number.

Almost half the people of the world live in towns and cities.

All over the world, women usually live longer than men.

There are 189 countries in the world. Each country has its own government, flag, capital city and money.

The biggest country in the world is Russia. It covers more than 17 million square kilometres.

America

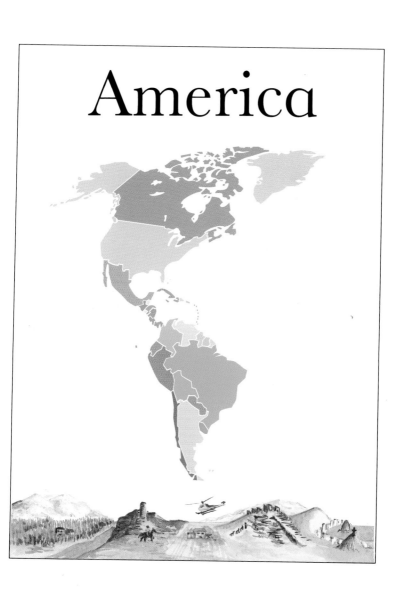

The frozen north

The far north of Canada is one of the coldest places on Earth. This is where the Inuits live.

Everyone wears warm clothes to keep out the icy cold. Planes bring food and other supplies for the winter.

Sledges pulled by dogs are a good way to get around. But people also drive skidoos.

Rubbing noses is the Inuit way of kissing.

This man is fishing through a hole
in the ice. Close by is the
igloo he has built for
shelter from the cold.
Although the igloo
is made of ice,
it is warm inside.
Inuits use the
igloos only when
they go fishing in
the winter.

31

Land of forests

Vast forests stretch across Canada, which is the second biggest country in the world. The forests supply trees for timber.

Lumberjacks cut down the trees with chainsaws. Logging trucks haul the trees to the sawmills, to be cut into planks of timber.

People in Canada and the United States love to eat maple syrup in cakes or on pancakes. The syrup comes from maple trees. At the end of winter, snow still covers the ground. The maple trees have no leaves. Now is the time to drill holes in the tree trunk. The watery sap inside the tree drips out into a bucket. Then the sap is carried to a cabin called the sugarhouse, and boiled. It turns into a sticky, sweet syrup. Delicious!

An Indian festival

The Indians were the first people to live in America. They still celebrate their ancient festivals. These Pueblo Indians of the United States are dancing to celebrate the Maize Festival.

The dancers wear special costumes and wear corn cobs on their heads. They sing to make the rain fall and bring them a good harvest.

When Pueblo children play with wooden kachina dolls, they learn about Indian history and legends. Each doll is painted to represent a magical spirit of the earth, sky or water. This is a winged spirit doll. It represents a spirit of the sky.

This Pueblo medicine man is trying to heal someone who is ill. He draws signs in the sand. His helpers chant songs.

City streets

The United States of America is home to many people whose parents, grand-parents, great grandparents or great-great grandparents came from other countries.

Many Americans live in big cities. These children play basketball in the street. Perhaps they dream of becoming sports stars one day.

Skyscrapers are the tallest buildings in the world. They tower above the busy streets.

A cattle ranch

As well as cities, there are wide open spaces in the United States. American farmers raise cattle on big farms called ranches. Cowboys look after the cattle.

This cowboy uses a rope called a lasso to catch a stray from the herd. He is an expert rider, and his horse is well trained to gallop and twist and turn.

After a long, tiring day on horseback, the cowboys relax around a campfire.

These children
are helping to
look after the
baby animals.

Some farms are so big that farmers use
helicopters as well as horses and jeeps.
Huge combine harvesters cut the wheat.

39

In the Caribbean

harvesting
bananas

The people of the Caribbean live on islands known as the West Indies. It is warm all year round, with lots of sunshine. Tourists visit the islands, to enjoy the beaches and the mountain scenery.

Many of the islanders are fishermen. They go out in small boats and catch fish in the warm waters around the islands. When they return with their catch, they pull their boats up onto the beach near the village and sell their fish. Later they spread out their nets to dry. This fisherman is mending his nets in the shade of a coconut palm.

A town square

It is noon, the hottest part of the day, so the square is almost empty. The people of this small town in Mexico are taking a break from work. They rest in the cool shade under the arches. It is pleasant to eat in the open air – a plate of tasty beans with pancakes called tortillas, or sweetcorn roasted on the cob.

Every town has its own fiesta or festival once a year. Then people fill the square.

During the fiesta, there are fireworks and music and dancing. Children try to break open a pot called the piñata, to get the sweets inside.

Market day

The people of the Andes Mountains live in one of the highest places in the world. Only the Himalayas in Asia are higher. It can be cold in the mountains so people wear clothes made from sheep and llama wool which is dyed in bright colours.

On market day everyone comes to town. Women carry their babies in shawls tied around their shoulders. People from the mountain farms come in trucks or on foot with their animals. They bring vegetables such as beans, yams and potatoes to sell in the street. They buy cooking pots and tools to take home.

Indians of the Amazon

The Amazon Indians live in the biggest rainforest in the world. It is hot and wet, and the forest is very thick. There are hardly any roads. People live in villages in small clearings. They grow vegetables, and the forest supplies them with everything else they need.

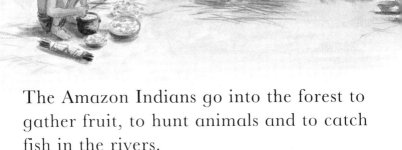

The Amazon Indians go into the forest to gather fruit, to hunt animals and to catch fish in the rivers.

Hunters go off into the
forest for a day or so.
This man is hunting
fish with a bow and
arrow.

Children help too.
They look after babies and gather food.

Music in Brazil

Much of the Amazon forest is in Brazil, the biggest country in South America. But most Brazilians live in cities. There is a famous carnival every year in the city of Rio de Janeiro. People come out into the streets and dance to the music.

There are bands playing in the street all year round. These drummers play tall African drums called bongos and old oil-drums called batucadas. Two men are dancing to the music.

Amazing facts

Christopher Columbus sailed from Spain to the Caribbean in 1492. He called the people of this 'New World' Indians, because he thought he had reached the East Indies of Asia.

After Columbus' voyage, many people from Spain came to Mexico. Mexicans still speak Spanish. Brazilians speak Portuguese because most of the people who came to Brazil were from Portugal.

Mexico City is the most crowded city in the world. More than 20 million people live there.

The tallest building in the world is in America. It is the Sears Tower in Chicago.

The maple leaf is the national symbol of Canada. It appears on Canada's flag.

Europe

In Scandinavia

Far up in the North are the Scandinavian countries of Finland, Sweden and Norway.

Scandinavia has cold, snowy winters. Ice covers the lakes and ponds. Sometimes the sea freezes over too. So people drill holes in the ice when they go fishing. They get out their sledges and skates. Hundreds of people take part in cross-country ski races.

Summers are warmer. Holiday-makers drive
out of town to the lakes and forests. They
take hot steam baths called saunas inside a
wooden cabin. To cool off, they go
swimming in the lake.

A fishing village

On the edge of the Atlantic Ocean, fishing has always been important. These pictures show a fishing community in Brittany, which is a region of France. The fishermen go out to sea in large boats called trawlers.

The trawlers drag nets through the water to catch sole, sardines and tuna. The fishermen pack the fish in boxes, with ice to keep them fresh. They stay at sea for several days. Then they return to their home port.

The boxes of fish are unloaded and sold in the fish market. Tourists on holiday come to watch.

The people of Brittany are called Bretons. Some Breton women still make and wear the traditional costume with lace caps.

A city in Europe

Most of the people of Europe live and work in towns and cities. Some European towns are small. Others have grown over many years into big cities.

There are public gardens and parks for everyone to enjoy. Sometimes a band comes to play on the bandstand.

The centre of the city is often the business area, with offices, banks and shops. Side by side, buildings old and new tell the history of the city.

Visitors and townspeople can
have a drink and a meal at
a café in the square.

If the weather is fine, it's fun to sit and
watch the world pass by.

Farming in Europe

On a small farm in Poland, everyone gets up early to help. There are fields to plough, crops to plant and pick, cows to milk and chickens to feed.

Farming is hard work. On the large farms, farmers use machines to help get the work done more quickly.

Europe's farmers grow a lot of wheat. They use combine harvesters to gather in the crop at harvest time, towards the end of summer.

Then they use tractors to plough the fields and sow more wheat.

Farmers also keep cattle, for milk and meat. Some of the milk is made into butter, cream, yoghurt and cheese.

A mountain village

The Alps are Europe's most famous mountains. In winter they are covered with snow. This mountain village in Switzerland becomes crowded. It is the skiing season. People come to the Alps on skiing holidays. They take a ski lift up the mountain, and then they ski down.

In summer, much of the snow melts and the skiers have gone.

Now cows can graze in green pastures high on the Alps. They give rich milk. Bees find pollen in the meadow flowers and make honey in their hives.

The skiers will be back with the snow next winter.

In Spain

Some parts of Europe have much warmer climates than others. In Spain and other countries in the south, it is warm enough to grow grapes. The grapes ripen in the hot summer sun. In September they are ready to be harvested.

Now the workers cut bunches
of grapes from the vines and
load them into baskets. The
grapes are taken to a press
and made into wine. At the
end of a good harvest, the
grape growers and the
winemakers all celebrate
together with a feast.

63

Islands in the sun

For a warm, sunny holiday, many Europeans go to Greece and its islands.

Some of the islanders make their living by fishing from small boats.

In summer, the days are long and hot.
People are glad of the shade in narrow
streets. They sit and talk at tables outside
small cafés.

Because there is so
much heat and very
little rain, much of
the land is dry. But
farmers grow good
crops of olives and
walnuts. They also
keep goats and sheep. A donkey is useful
for carrying small loads.

65

A gypsy festival

Gypsies have travelled around Europe for hundreds of years. Once they lived in caravans pulled by horses. Now most gypsies have motor homes. But they still love horses. And many still speak the old gypsy language called Romany.
Every May, gypsies gather from all over Europe for a great religious festival.

The festival is held in Saintes-Maries de la Mer, in the South of France. For two days, people sing and dance and play music together. A procession goes to the seashore to bathe two statues of saints.

Amazing facts

The biggest city in Europe is Moscow, Russia's capital city.

Europe's most watery city is Venice in Italy. Venice is built on the edge of the sea. It has more canals than streets, so people often travel about in boats instead of cars and buses.

Europe is the second smallest of the Earth's continents. Yet only Asia has more people.

Twelve countries belong to the European Union or European Community. Other countries are waiting to join.

Africa

Going to market

In North Africa, in the country of Morocco, the old part of town is called the medina. People going to market pass through a large gateway into the medina. They come to buy food, jewellery, pots and carpets. Each trade has its own market in its own street, called the souk.

This man is a tanner or leatherworker. He soaks animal skins in dye to colour them. Other people use the leather to make bags and shoes to sell.

Desert travellers

The Sahara is one of the hottest places to live. The Tuareg are nomads who wander the desert with their camels and goats.

They live in tents which they can pack up and load onto their camels.

The Tuareg set off with their camels in a caravan, with one camel following another. A camel driver leads the caravan across the desert. He knows the best way to the next stopping place. At night, he finds the way by looking at the stars.

It hardly ever rains in the Sahara. Camels can go for days without water, but people need water every day.

So the Tuareg fetch water from wells and carry it with them in goatskin containers.

73

Beside the River Nile

The Nile is Africa's longest river. It flows right through Egypt. Egypt's farmers grow wheat and vegetables in fields beside the river. Without water from the Nile, the land would be a desert like the Sahara.

Farmers dig irrigation canals and ditches to carry the Nile's water to their crops. Day and night, oxen turn the waterwheels that keep the water flowing.

Sailing boats called feluccas carry people and goods up and down the Nile.

A town in Africa

Towns begin as places where people meet to trade. Many of the large African towns are ports near the sea or by a river. So boats are just as useful as trucks.

Africa's towns are growing quickly. Some are now great cities, with tall skyscrapers.

More and more people are leaving country villages to live in towns. They go to find jobs in offices, shops and factories.

In the city of Dakar in West Africa, these
people are shopping in an open-air market.
Traders set out vegetables and spices, cloth
and other goods on the ground. There is
friendly arguing over prices. Women often
carry shopping home on their heads.

Village life

Villages in Africa can look very different from one another because people use different materials and build in different ways. The houses in this village on the Ivory Coast have thatched roofs.

The people of the village enjoy stories, gossip and games. Beneath a baobab tree, men are playing a game called awale. The two players move seeds around holes in a block of wood.

The women are preparing a meal together. They pound millet or cassava into flour for baking bread.

Some of the villagers are spinning cotton and weaving it into cloth on a loom.

79

Life on the water

This is a fishing village in on the coast of
Benin in West Africa. The houses are built
on stilts high above the water. There are no
streets, and people move about in small
boats. The men go out fishing every
morning. They throw out their nets and pull
in the catch.

After a morning's fishing, the men paddle
their boats back to the village. The women
hold a floating market. They sell the fresh
fish brought back in the boats. They buy
fruit and vegetables brought out from the
shore by traders.

Farming in Africa

In Central Africa, farmers grow rows and rows of tea bushes on the hillsides. These workers in Zaire carefully pick the best leaves from the bushes. The leaves are dried and crumbled, and shipped all over the world. They end up in the tea bags we use to make tea.

Farmers also grow coffee beans in Central and East Africa.

In the forests of Africa, bridges across the rivers are made of lianas or creepers. You need a good head for heights to cross this swaying bridge! It hangs from trees on each side of the river.

The River Congo flows through the vast rainforest of Zaire, to the Atlantic Ocean.

An ostrich farm

A very unusual kind of farm is found in South Africa. It is an ostrich farm! Ostriches are the biggest birds in the world. The males have magnificent feathers.

Ostriches cannot fly but they have powerful legs, so they can run fast and they are very strong. They can even carry people on their backs for a short distance. But watch out when an ostrich kicks!

Tourists come to ostrich farms to see the birds.

Keepers look after the flocks of ostriches on the farm. The female ostriches lay their huge eggs inside special shelters. One ostrich can lay as many as ten eggs. No other bird lays such large eggs.

When the chicks hatch, they soon run as fast as their parents.

Amazing facts

People lived in Africa over two million years ago. Now scientists have found the bones and footprints of even older human-like beings.

The Sahara was not always a sandy desert. It once had rivers and grasslands, and hippos and giraffes lived there.

Cairo in Egypt is Africa's biggest city. More than six million people live there.

Almost 700 million people live in Africa. There are 52 countries, and more than 800 different languages.

Asia

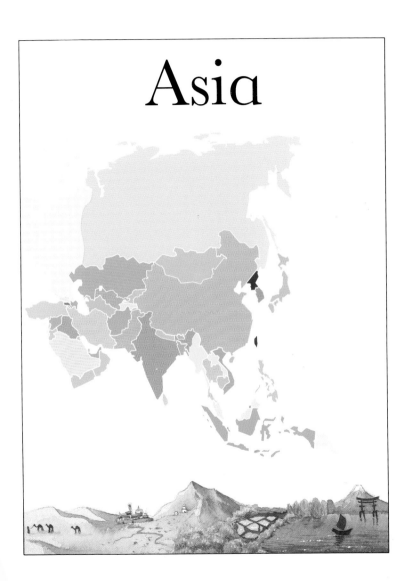

On a kibbutz

These children live in Israel. Their home is a farm called a kibbutz. They all live together as one large family.

Everyone works together on the kibbutz. The farmers have turned dry land into green fields and orchards. They grow vegetables and fruit for sale abroad.

These workers are picking oranges and putting them into crates.

Oil in the desert

Saudi Arabia is a hot, dry place. Bedouin and other nomads cross the Arabian Desert on their camels. Beneath the sand there is oil. Engineers drill wells deep underground to reach the oil. Then road tankers and pipes carry the oil to ships waiting at the coast. The Arab countries sell their oil to the rest of the world.

In town and in the desert, men wear loose robes and a head-dress called a keffiyah. Most of the women wear a veil.

In the desert and up in the mountains, people hunt with falcons and dogs, just as their ancestors did. This man holds the falcon on his wrist, and at the right moment he launches the bird towards its prey.

In Afghanistan

Afghanistan has deserts, mountains, and plains

In the plains to the north, Afghan horsemen play an exciting game called bozkashi. The ball is a blown-up goatskin. One rider grabs it and carries it. The other players try to take it from him.

A covered market or bazaar is sheltered from the summer sun and the winter snow. People come to the bazaar from far-off mountain villages to buy and sell goods.

Among the Mongols

The nomads of Mongolia wander the grassy plains with their sheep, goats, cattle, camels and horses. They carry their homes with them. A Mongol family's home is a tent called a yurt. It is built with wooden poles and covered with felt cloth. The felt is made of wool from the family's animals.

The felt keeps out sun, wind and rain. So a yurt is cool in summer and warm in winter.

This Mongol family prepare
a meal inside their yurt.
When it is time to move on,
they will take apart the
yurt, roll it all up and take
it with them.

Mongol children learn
to ride when they are
toddlers. They become
excellent horsemen.

The old Mongol way of life is changing.
Many Mongols are no longer nomads. They
stay in one place, on farms or in towns. But
often they still live in a yurt.

China, Asia's giant

To the south of Mongolia lies China, the giant of Asia. China has more people than any other country in the world.

Many Chinese start the day by doing tai-chi exercises. Then they go off to work, on foot or by bike. In the busy streets people are selling snacks and vegetables, playing chess and mah-jong and reading the news.

A monastery

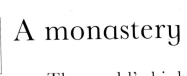

The world's highest mountains are in the Himalayas. On the slopes of the mountains are monasteries where monks follow the teachings of Buddha. They pray and they study, far from the noise and crowds of city life.

In the country of Bhutan, some boys train to be monks from seven years of age. They wear simple robes of yellow or orange. They learn the prayers and holy chants, and they watch the religious ceremonies.

A holy river

The River Ganges is the greatest river in India. Hindus believe it is a holy river. On its banks are Hindu temples. People visit the city of Varanasi to bathe in the Ganges.

Crowds of Hindu pilgrims gather at dawn on the steps leading down to the Ganges. They bathe in the river to make themselves pure. They pray, and drink a mouthful of water.

Cows wander about the streets of Indian cities. Hindus believe that cows are sacred animals. People do not harm them.

Religion is important in India. There are festivals and holidays throughout the year. Not all the people of India are Hindus. There are also Muslims, Sikhs, Jains and Christians.

The rice growers

All over Southeast Asia people grow and eat a lot of rice. Rice is a kind of grass. It needs warmth and lots of water to grow well. Farmers plough the fields, and then flood them with water from a canal or a river. Buffalo are better than tractors for this kind of farming.

On this farm in Thailand, rice plants are carefully grown from seed in special nursery fields. Then they are planted out in flooded fields called paddy fields.

After three months, the rice is ready to harvest. The field is drained dry. The farmers cut the stems and store the rice grains in granaries.

Gifts for the gods

Bali is one of the many islands of Indonesia. These women offer gifts to the gods, so that the gods will protect their villages and homes, and bring them good luck. They carry on their heads gifts of rice, fruit and flowers. Children join in the procession.

The Balinese love
dancing. They start
when they are very
young. At the age of
ten, girls can dance in
the ceremonies. But it
takes years to learn
all the dance
movements.

105

In Japan

About 120 million people live on the islands of Japan. Indoors, the Japanese take off their shoes. The floor is covered with tatamis, which are mats made of plaited rice straw.

At mealtimes, the family kneels around the table.

In the morning, everyone rolls up their futon, or mattress bed, and puts it away.

karate

kendo

judo

The Japanese are good at martial arts.
In kendo, two people fight with staves.
They wear helmets to protect themselves.

In karate and
judo, they fight
with bare hands
and feet.

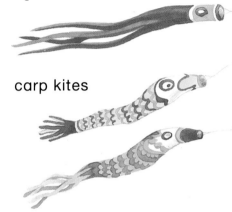
carp kites

During the
children's festival
on 5th May, kites
shaped like fish fly
high in the sky.

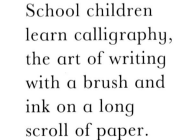

calligraphy

School children
learn calligraphy,
the art of writing
with a brush and
ink on a long
scroll of paper.

People of Papua

Papua New Guinea is a land of mountains and forests. The people are called Papuans. For important feasts, Papuan men paint their faces and wear necklaces of pigs' teeth.

The Papuans live in large villages, in houses made from woven reeds.

They keep pigs and chickens and they look after vegetable gardens.

They grow sweet potatoes, yams and taro. They also harvest bananas and coconuts.

The men hunt and fish. They make their bows and arrows from split bamboo and sharpened stones. They also carve axe heads from stones, to sell to tourists. Boys and girls learn their parents' skills by helping them. Some children go to school, but others live in remote mountain areas with no roads or schools.

More than 700 different languages are spoken in Papua New Guinea.

Amazing facts

Asia is the biggest of all the continents. Six out of every ten people in the world live in Asia.

China has more than 1,100 million people. That's more than any other country. Next comes India, with about 850 million people.

The world's highest mountain, Mount Everest, is in Asia, in the Himalayas.

Indonesia in Southeast Asia is a country made up of more than 13,000 islands.

The biggest city in Asia is Tokyo, the capital of Japan.

New Guinea is the second biggest island in the world. Only Greenland is bigger.

Oceania

A sheep farm

Australia has some of the biggest farms in the world. The sheep stations are so big that farmers use planes, trucks, motorbikes and horses to get around. At shearing time, the sheep are rounded up into sheds to have their wool cut off.

Cattle stations have huge herds of cattle.

This farm is far from the nearest town and school. So the farm children have lessons at home. They listen to their teacher over the radio.

If someone is ill, the flying doctor comes out to the farm by plane.

People of the outback

Australia is the home of the Aborigines. They were the first people to live there. Nowadays many Aborigines live in towns or work on farms.

Other Aborigines still live in the dry wilderness called the outback.

Aborigines can find food and water even in a desert. They hunt kangaroos and other animals with spears. They also hunt with curved boomerangs which they carve from wood.

kangaroo

This artist paints the animals of the outback and the old Aboriginal legends. He paints with coloured earths and burnt wood, on a piece of bark from the eucalyptus tree.

In New Zealand

In the Pacific Ocean to the east of Australia lies New Zealand. It has two main islands and thousands of smaller ones. So the sea is never far away, even when you live in a city. It's fun to go out in a yacht or a motor boat.

Up in the mountains, the North Island is famous for its volcanic mud pools and hot springs called geysers.

New Zealanders are keen on sport, especially rugby, cricket and bowls. People meet at this bowls club for a game and a chat.

Polynesian islanders

Scattered across the Pacific Ocean are the tiny islands of Polynesia. The islanders live in villages beside the sea. They go fishing in canoes. They beat the water with their paddles to make the fish rise to the surface. Then they catch them with spears.

Tall coconut palms grow everywhere. Coconuts are good to eat, with a milky drink inside. The nut also gives coconut oil. The hairy fibre around the nut can be made into rope. And the tree trunk can be hollowed out and made into a canoe. What a useful plant!

In the clear waters of the coral reef,
swimmers find colourful fish and shells.

It's all part of our beautiful world.

Amazing facts

Australia is the only country which is also a continent.

Australia has the world's biggest coral reef, the Great Barrier Reef. The reef is more than 2,000 kilometres long.

Australia and New Zealand are part of the huge region called Oceania, in the Pacific Ocean. Oceania has thousands of other islands, some of them very small. The island of Nauru covers an area of just 21 square kilometres.

People came to the Pacific islands from Asia thousands of years ago. The Maoris were the first people to live in New Zealand.

INDEX